EDGE BOOKS™

STARS OF PRO WRESTLING

★ ★ ★ ★ ★ ★ ★ ★

MATT HARDY

BY JASON D. NEMETH

Consultant:
Mike Johnson, Writer
PWInsider.com

CAPSTONE PRESS
a capstone imprint

Edge Books are published by Capstone Press,
151 Good Counsel Drive, P.O. Box 669, Mankato, Minnesota 56002.
www.capstonepub.com

122010
006037R

Library of Congress Cataloging-in-Publication Data
Nemeth, Jason D.
    Matt Hardy / by Jason Nemeth.
    p. cm. — (Edge books. stars of pro wrestling.)
    Includes bibliographical references and index.
    Summary: "Describes the life and career of pro wrestler Matt Hardy" —
Provided by publisher.
    ISBN 978-1-4296-3946-0 (library binding)
    1. Hardy, Matt, 1973 or 4– — Juvenile literature. 2. Wrestlers — United
States — Biography — Juvenile literature. I. Title.
GV1196.H32N46 2010
796.812092 — dc22   2009027261

Editorial Credits
Kathryn Clay, editor; Kyle Grenz, designer; Jo Miller, media researcher;
    Laura Manthe, production specialist

Photo Credits
Alamy/Miguel Pereira, 24
DoD photo by PO1 Kristin Fitzsimmons, USN, 11
Getty Images Inc./WireImage/Bob Levey, 17, 29; Bobby Bank, 9
Globe Photos/John Barrett, 12, 21; Paul Skipper, 15
Newscom, 13, 18, 25, 27; Icon Sports Media/CITYFILES/Alexandre Pona, 6;
    WENN/Carrie Devorah, 23
Wikimedia/Creative Commons/Mshake3, 5
Zuma Press/Icon SMI/Tom 'Mo' Moschella, cover

Design Elements
Shutterstock/amlet; Henning Janos; J. Danny; kzww

TABLE OF CONTENTS

Chapter 1

SCRAMBLE FOR THE BELT

Matt Hardy entered the ring at Unforgiven 2008. The first-ever **Scramble Match** for a world wrestling title was about to begin. The Extreme Championship Wrestling (ECW) title was on the line. Matt's first opponent was The Miz.

Matt put The Miz in a headlock and tried for an early pinfall. But The Miz escaped, and the two men fought back and forth. Then The Miz performed his **signature move**, a *Reality Check*, on Matt. But Matt rolled out of the ring before The Miz could pin him. By the time Matt was pulled back into the ring, the clock was counting down.

Scramble Match — a 20-minute wrestling match; two wrestlers start the match, and another wrestler joins every five minutes.

signature move — the move for which a wrestler is best known

Matt Hardy has wrestled professionally for more than 10 years.

WRESTLING MOVE

Reality Check — a running knee strike followed by a neck breaker

Chavo Guerrero entered the ring at the five-minute mark. He knocked The Miz over the top rope and performed a *Frog Splash* on Matt. Matt recovered and *clotheslined* The Miz. Then he pinned Guerrero. Matt was the new ECW champion, but now he had to defend his title for the rest of the match.

Mark Henry (left) uses his size to crush opponents.

Ten minutes into the match, Mark Henry entered the ring. Henry is called the World's Strongest Man. Guerrero, The Miz, and Matt all looked worried as the 400-pound (181-kilogram) wrestler approached. They ganged up on Henry and backed him into a corner. Henry pushed down all three men like they were toys. He clotheslined each of them and lifted Matt over his head. Matt fell face-first onto the canvas. Then Henry slammed Guerrero and covered him for the count of three. Henry was now the ECW champion, and he seemed unstoppable.

Matt tried to jump on Henry from the ropes but was pushed out of the ring. When Matt tried to jump at Henry again, he was caught in midair. Henry put Matt in a crushing bear hug. Matt's chances of winning grew dimmer with each tick of the clock.

WRESTLING MOVES

Frog Splash — a wrestler jumps off the ropes and brings his arms and legs toward his body and out again before landing

clothesline — a wrestler runs toward the opponent with his arm outstretched and smashes his arm into the opponent's neck

Chapter 2

A TRAMPOLINE AND A DREAM

Matt Hardy was born September 23, 1974, in Cameron, North Carolina. His brother, Jeff, who is also a pro wrestler, was born three years later. When Matt was only 12 years old, his mother, Ruby, died from cancer. After her death, their father, Gilbert, raised Matt and Jeff.

Gilbert Hardy knew the value of hard work. He worked long hours as a farmer. He wanted Matt and Jeff to grow up and get jobs with the U.S. government. But the boys wanted to be pro wrestlers.

When Gilbert bought his sons a trampoline in 1987, Matt and Jeff roped it in using garden hoses. They turned the trampoline into a wrestling ring using trees for ring posts. The brothers spent hours practicing wrestling moves they saw on TV. Matt especially liked the high-flying stunts of the Rockers. This tag team featured Shawn Michaels and Marty Jannetty.

Jeff and Matt (left to right) have won many championship belts.

Matt and Jeff dreamed of being pro wrestlers. Even though their father disapproved, Matt and Jeff started performing at local fairs. Eventually they met wrestler Gary Sabaugh, known as the Italian Stallion. Sabaugh ran a North Carolina wrestling **promotion**. In 1993, he gave Matt and Jeff their professional **debuts** in the World Wrestling Federation (WWF). The WWF is now called World Wrestling Entertainment (WWE). Matt was only 19 years old.

OMEGA

Even with Sabaugh's help, Matt and Jeff were far from being WWF superstars. Matt started his own promotion to help their careers. He called it the Organization of Modern Extreme Grappling Arts (OMEGA).

WRESTLING FACT

While wrestling for OMEGA, Matt's wrestling name was Surge.

Shane Helms was signed by WCW in 2002.

Running his own promotion meant Matt, with Jeff's help, had a lot of work to do. The brothers didn't just wrestle. They set up and took down the ring. They designed costumes for the wrestlers. They even advertised their shows and sold tickets. Many of the wrestlers who joined OMEGA went on to professional careers. Shane "Hurricane" Helms, who wrestles in WWE, got his start in OMEGA.

promotion — a wrestling company
debut — a first public appearance

Wrestling Promotions

OMEGA was not the first wrestling promotion Matt and Jeff put together. Their very first promotion was actually called Teen Wrestling Foundation (TWF).

TWF was later changed to stand for the Trampoline Wrestling Foundation. After that, Matt and Jeff created the East Coast Wrestling Foundation (ECWF). When they added a business partner, they changed the name to the New Frontier Wrestling Alliance (NFWA).

During this time, Matt and Jeff made more than 50 videos of their matches. They even brought them to local video stores so their fans could rent them.

Matt and Jeff (left to right) enjoy being in front of the camera.

Stone Cold Steve Austin defeated jobbers like Matt.

Matt's hard work caught the attention of the WWF. He spent a few years as a **jobber**, wrestling stars like Nikolai Volkoff, Triple H, and Stone Cold. In 1998, Matt and Jeff were invited to a training camp taught by former wrestler Dory Funk Jr. After training with Funk, both Matt and Jeff were offered WWF contracts.

jobber — a wrestler who continually loses his or her matches; this is usually done to help the image of another wrestler.

Chapter 3

EXTREME MOVES

When Matt and Jeff were boys, they performed dangerous stunts, including a 20-foot (6-meter) cliff dive into a lake. They also raced dirt bikes and climbed the tall trees in their backyard.

As they practiced wrestling moves on their trampoline, they copied the flips and dives they saw on TV. When Matt and Jeff became pro wrestlers, they continued these daredevil moves. They were known for jumping off the top rope, flipping from ladders, and crashing through tables. All of these stunts helped earn Matt and Jeff the nickname Team Extreme. It wasn't easy on their bodies, but it helped make them famous.

Lita joined Team Extreme in 2000.

THE LADDER MATCH

In 1999, The Hardy Boyz faced Edge and Christian in the first-ever Tag Team Ladder Match. High above the ring hung $100,000. Whoever reached it first won the money and the match.

Edge and Christian immediately knocked down the Hardys and tried to get the ladders. The Hardys threw Edge into the ropes. As he bounced off, they elbowed him in the face. Edge went after a ladder again, but Matt tackled him onto the stadium floor.

As Matt brought a ladder into the ring, Christian jumped off the top rope. He landed on Matt and knocked him out of the ring. Christian was almost to the top of a ladder when Jeff threw him off. When Edge got halfway up, Matt tipped the ladder over. Christian used the ladder to hit Matt in the stomach. As Christian tried to climb up the ladder, Matt performed a *suplex* off the ladder. All this happened in the first seven minutes of a 20-minute match.

WRESTLING MOVES

suplex — a wrestler lifts his opponent over his shoulder and falls backward, driving the opponent's back into the mat

The wrestlers continued to battle back and forth. Finally, all four wrestlers were climbing up two ladders at once. They punched and kicked each other as they climbed. Matt and Christian got knocked off one ladder. Then Jeff pushed Edge off the other ladder. Jeff made it to the money and grabbed a victory for the Hardy Boyz.

Jeff shows off his high-flying moves during a ladder match.

Matt worked hard to be a successful singles wrestler.

Wrestling Without a Partner

For the first three years of his wrestling career, Matt was known as one half of the Hardy Boyz. Together he and Jeff won six tag team championship titles. Years later they would team up once more for a seventh title win. In 2007, Matt wrestled with MVP for an eighth win.

But Matt didn't want to share the spotlight with his younger brother. He wanted to be known as a great singles wrestler as well. He already had some success. Matt held the Hardcore Championship briefly. He also held the European Championship. But he decided to set his sights higher. In 2002, he broke up the Hardy Boyz to wrestle alone.

Chapter 4

SINGLES CAREER

One of the first belts Matt went after was the Cruiserweight Championship. To qualify for this title, he had to weigh 220 pounds (100 kilograms) or less. Matt went on a diet and worked out for weeks. Eventually he made the weight and got a title shot.

He defeated Billy Kidman at No Way Out 2003 and held on to the title for four months. It was a great success, but it would be five years before Matt held another singles belt.

WRESTLING FACT

Matt's brother, Jeff, won the WWE Championship Belt at Armageddon 2008. With that win, they became the first brothers of modern wrestling to hold major titles at the same time.

In 2003, Matt began calling himself Matt Hardy: Version 1.0.

TROUBLED TIMES

Matt took time off in August 2004 for knee surgery. At the time, Matt was dating WWE wrestler Lita. But while he was recovering, Lita started dating Edge. Matt was angry and wrote about his feelings online. WWE fired Matt in April 2005 for mixing up his business and personal life.

Matt was devastated. His wrestling dream and the woman he loved were both gone. But Matt's fans didn't forget about him. They booed Edge at matches. More than 15,000 fans supported Matt by signing a petition. The petition convinced the WWE to rehire Matt in August 2005.

Once he returned, Matt and Edge **feuded** for months. During one cage match at Unforgiven 2005, Matt climbed to the top of a steel cage. He jumped and landed on Edge for the win. Matt admitted later that it was a bad idea. He hurt his spine and lower back when he landed.

feud — a long-running quarrel

U.S. CHAMPIONSHIP

Matt's career picked up again in 2007. Matt had teamed with MVP to win a tag championship. But MVP thought he was better than Matt. The two wrestlers competed against each other in different contests. MVP tried to outdo Matt in arm wrestling, push-ups, and pizza eating. Then Matt went after MVP's U.S. Championship belt. At Backlash 2008, he beat MVP for the title. With that success, Matt decided to wrestle for his first world championship. His chance came at Unforgiven 2008.

Matt feuded with Edge for much of 2005.

THE FINAL FIVE MINUTES OF UNFORGIVEN 2008

For five minutes, Mark Henry dominated the Unforgiven match. But then Fit Finlay charged into the ring. Finlay was the fifth·and final wrestler in the scramble match. He attacked Henry in a fury. He grabbed Henry's head and drove it into the mat. He tried for a pin, but Henry threw him off.

Mark Henry was a weightlifter before joining WWE.

Hornswoggle (left) helped
Finlay (right) win matches.

When Henry put Finlay in a bear hug,
it seemed like no one could stop him. But
Hornswoggle, Finlay's sidekick, entered the
ring and distracted the referee. Finlay grabbed
his cane and smacked it over Henry's head.
Matt helped Finlay throw Henry over the top
rope. Then Finlay pinned Matt. With less than
four minutes to go in the match, Finlay was the
new champion.

The Miz came back and drop-kicked Finlay from the top rope. Matt used his signature move, the *Twist of Fate*, on The Miz and got the three count. Matt was the champion for the second time. There were only three minutes left in the match.

Now Matt played defense. He had to prevent anyone else from getting a pinfall. Henry went after the wrestlers one at a time. He slammed them to the mat and tried to cover them. Matt attacked him each time to stop the pin. Matt stopped 12 pin attempts in three minutes. When 20 minutes were up, he was the official ECW champion.

Matt used the Twist of Fate to defeat opponents such as MVP.

WRESTLING MOVE

Twist of Fate — to put the opponent in a front facelock before twisting and dropping to the mat

WHAT THE FUTURE HOLDS

With his success so far, Matt has made his father proud. Gilbert watches both his sons on TV. He even bought action figures of Matt and Jeff. But his sons aren't finished yet.

Although Matt has already won the ECW Championship, there are still titles that he has not yet won. These titles include the World Heavyweight Championship and the WWE Championship. He may try for those.

Matt is keeping his career options open. In 2003, he wrote a book with Jeff about their early career called *Exist 2 Inspire*. He said he'd like to write another book on his own. Whatever Matt chooses to do, he's sure to do it with superstar style.

Jeff and Matt (left to right) have wrestled each other in singles matches.

GLOSSARY ★ ★ ★ ★ ★

debut (day-BYOO) — a first public appearance

feud (FYOOD) — a long-running quarrel between two people or groups of people

jobber (JOB-uhr) — a wrestler who continually loses his or her matches; this is usually done to help the image of another wrestler.

petition (puh-TISH-uhn) — a letter signed by many people asking those in power to change their policy or actions

promotion (pruh-MOH-shuhn) — a wrestling company

Scramble Match (SKRAM-buhl MACH) — a 20-minute wrestling match; two wrestlers start the match, and another wrestler joins every five minutes

signature move (SIG-nuh-chur MOOV) — the move for which a wrestler is best known; this move is also called a finishing move.

tag team (TAG TEEM) — when two wrestlers partner together against other teams

Nemeth, Jason D. *Edge.* Stars of Pro Wrestling. Mankato, Minn.: Capstone Press, 2010.

Shields, Brian, and Kevin Sullivan. *WWE Encyclopedia.* New York: DK Publishing, 2009.

INTERNET SITES

FactHound offers a safe, fun way to find Internet sites related to this book. All of the sites on FactHound have been researched by our staff.

Here's all you do:

Visit *www.facthound.com*

FactHound will fetch the best sites for you!

INDEX ★ ★ ★ ★ ★ ★ ★